Rembrandt's Smock

Lynn Strongin

Plain View Press
P. O. 42255
Austin, TX 78704

plainviewpress.net
sb@plainviewpress.net
512-441-2452

Copyright Lynn Strongin, 2007. All rights reserved.
ISBN: 978-1-891386-82-4
Library of Congress Number: 2007927508

Cover: Wim Blom, *Blue Dipper* (© 2001), oil on canvas 38 x 54 cm (15 x 21 1/4")

Acknowledgments

Some of these poems appeared, at times in slightly different versions, in *The American Voice, The Antigonish Review, The Argotist Online, Avatar Review, Big Bridges, Blue Mesa Review, The Galley Sail Review, Identity Theory, Island, New Works Review, Outsider's Ink, Painted Bride Quarterly, Pemmican, Prairie Schooner, Prism International, Right Hand Pointing, Rivendell Review, Shenandoah, Snow Monkey, Solo Magazine, Stooge,* and *Sunrust.*

"Make Hay While the Sun Shines" and "You Have Started Up This Foxy Engine" appear in *You Can Always Find Yourself by the Moon,* an online chapbook by Beard of Bees (beardofbees.com, 2005).

"Lithograph of Amherst" appears in *Visiting Emily: Poems Inspired by the Life & Work of Emily Dickinson* ed. Thom Tamarro (University of Iowa Press, 2002).

"Theresienstadt" will appear in *Blood to Remember: American Poets on the Holocaust,* ed Charles Fishman, Time Being Books (2007).

Contents

Jeremiah Weather 7

    Federico's Lamb 9
    Fire in rock-maple 11
    Prayers On Palestrina Street 12
    Driving Home 13
    The Unknowing: Immigrant 14
    Cider Apples 15
    Christina's World 16
    Burn 17
    Chilled 18
    Winter 19
    A green twilight after rain 20
    Dark Salt 21
    The Six-Sided Snowflake 22
    The City Is Wax Combs 23
    All Giving Things 24
    Seeing Eye 25
    This Is No Breughel Day 26
    Soon the week will be upon us 27
    Jeremiah-Weather 28
    The Hellish Light Or Coppery 29
    Civil War Soldier 30
    Firstborn / Lastborn 32
    What a Waste Of World 33
    Theresienstadt 35
    Help My Unbelief 37

Short Visiting Hours For Children 41

    Short Visiting Hours For Children 43
    Multiplication 45
    Opaque disease 47
    Time taken at the flood 48
    Buckled 49
    Unroped 50
    I Wish To God Your Depression Were a Lake 52
    Pneumonia 53
    Second Notification 54

100%	55	
They are trying a new chemical		56
You have started up this foxy engine		57
Make hay while the sun shines	58	
Shaker Box, Broom, Clock	60	
Living On One Lung	62	
Hollyhock	64	

Rembrandt's Smock   65

When Winter Comes	67	
Lithograph Of Amherst	68	
A Few Canvases	69	
This Wired World	70	
Photographs Of Albatrosses	71	
Brightwork / Ave	72	
Danish geese,	74	
Bringing the tower-ravens in	75	
Horsefall Backward Slow Motion	76	
Boy With Ball	78	
Frost Flowers	80	
Blood was red Mississippi daybreak	81	
When you consider that freedom is an illusion		82
Rembrandt's Smock	83	
About the Author	89	

*for my mother, the painter, in memoriam
and for Deborah, photographer*

Marguerite Strongin, Portrait (1941), oil on canvas, 51 cm x 61 cm (24" x 20")

Jeremiah Weather

I know noble accents
And lucid, inescapable rhythms;
But I know, too,
That the blackbird is involved
In what I know.

Wallace Stevens, *Thirteen Ways Of Looking*
At a Blackbird

Federico's Lamb

              i.

In a wire basket poems collect dust diamonds:
the blown box of the world gleams.

Kitchen window filling with pearl snow:
Federico's lamb in the bath window, blue soap in white sun.

In North Carolina, they're getting up breakfast & in Asheville, in
    Penobscot, Main,
in the Bible Belt & in the plains; in Nebraska, boiling neck bones of
    the lamb for broth.

Home, sky's the color of barley:
the tongue moves quicker than the brain.

Time for the translation out of freedom into work.

              ii.

Tallow curls thin to spunglass.

Sojourners canter in wind that sheets their bodies in layers of ice
making their own music.

One blue window covered with plastic in Rome, Georgia, sheltering
    Federico's lamb
head scrubbed down to a nugget.

Curls come, the kind only pencils sharpened make.

        iii.

Trouble renewing passports
moving back night like a panel over a painting.

It isn't debt alone
apart from that debt the world exacts & never pays back;

it's distinct quiet makes for the sombre mood coming:
these poems in a wire-basket collecting dust-diamonds:
the blown box of the world agleam.

Fire in rock-maple

woke me on the tilt-table:
bright as burning sugar.

Healing was a pipe-dream: Death had dropped me like a hot potato.
I reached out toward that filmic sugar-maple
to marry fire   bride that fiery autumn. In my head I
        composed poems,   alphabets of fire arching like wolfhounds.

What wedding!
Parishioners filed in:
wind our bridesmaid.

Even the uninvited came:
storm went weeding, that grim smiler with the knife.

What a witness is a kid!
Tamer & hawk,
slayer & slain.

            ○

Legs could no longer carry me to a tree.

After my sugarbush summer—Death was rule:
Life—the except-
ional raptor.

Prayers On Palestrina Street

The blind child opens a sleepy eye: fire of his hair flashes like red fur
in the oval mirror.
An old 1930's Packard named *Norman* in first brass tuba sun
    suggests
it's
down South
where boys are named Jebulum.

Girls traipse to First Communion in dresses with falling hems
like swanked up peacocks.

A *Reader's Digest*
life accompanies the blind boy's mother
humming on her way to the Magdalena Bakery next-door to the
    laundry.

Driving Home

Shopping centers turn dark.
There is something terrible about winter
in Iowa, Nebraska, wherever
you wait
for something you can't name.
But I believe
in that certain blue-violet
which enters the eye
when it sees something: a light switching on,
the last steely sun
hitting a shopping cart
running into another
in Des Moines,
or Butte, or wherever,
that drives home the wonder, the last supper
always going on
a block or two down
as light surrounds the dinner plates, in workman's revelation.

The Unknowing: Immigrant

It's not my face:
I had one grey eye, one green.
The grey eye
was like rain.
The green
like nothing else.
This being is as strange to me
as winter-starved deer, fed only the song
of the grouse rushing off,
the storm bearing down.

Cider Apples

The soul is at her window of flesh
lightly leaning on a green paint frame.
She
doesn't exist any more:
only her dark wit
bronze
lets her go on the inside of her hound.
She's in his skin.
She walks around the country.
A gull-rain & sun have bleached an old spruce stand.
She sees witching:
the core of New England.

Christina's World

The light bulb's a high-intensity thinker
hung.
For Christina,
paralyzed,
even the colors of light
shrink like a worm.
Flowered dresses match the rising sea.
Her hair is strong reddish, her eyes deep brown.
Years of confinement
smell of burning oil, charred wood.
Fat cats clot her room
and old cloth.
She gazes seaward.
Locks her look back to land.
In her mind there's a lake
bulb-sized
where energy's pent
in an unmoving green.

Burn

The sky is glass.
Brittle leaves.
There's the vase,
dried flowers in.
Her man crackles like fire,
as she looks for the gun.
Love is paying attention:
the house could burn down.

Chilled

Sledge & milk
in snow. The slow compassion.
I give you the red house,
calm after its fire
and the cool rope
uncoiled after the hanging.
A chorus of sparrows I give you:
no single sound
but the burning bodies, cooled,
of the foxes who swallowed the hound.

Winter

Ironmonger, all 4 sides rusted
train-spotter
         is
forging   tooling away at our spirits:
gray as the knifegrind.

One can hear gears lock & mesh
metal shearing in heaven:
a dog's nails scraping pitchpine.

But the bay
of twigs turns coppery   roosters' knobs afire Titian
     hair
and we are
     transported:
               water in a metal pail reflecting sky
               then frozen like sugar, blistering;
               last caramelized, cracked into ice for the holy wafer.

A green twilight after rain

filled up the
great bay   white wall-paper puffs from a black train.

As a child, one curled up by the wireless
listening to shipping forecasts:
sea-dogs in sou'westers battling church-high waves in Fogger and
    Disher.

Vestigial flowers   virginal
round my mother's pillow
who has been ambulanced into the E.R. with a broken hip, sent to
    rehabilitation,
threatened suicide,
now has pneumonia.

How much more, churchmouse, must you suffer?
And the knob, true brass bordered by glass, which I can turn
to open the door
page embroidered with wildflower.
Sweet pea sombred by the pain of leveling with faith each single
    breathing hour,
        & turning over & over every known thing.

Dark Salt

Blake's Jove
wielding his compass mane flowing, a lion.

There's a new strange bird on the porch.
Dark salt stands around,

magnetic "healing" words on the fridge.

We have corruptible prayers
incorruptible ones:
Some tarnish like silver salt cellars:
Sodium darkens a pillar rising in the
half-light,
a valentine shaped magnifier on the bureau of old
oak.

A soldier in my dream strikes a match flame on a
mannequin's hip.
Parallel train tracks in London mesmerize me:
Was I a train-spotter in a former incarnation?

A great bellow, a marrow of white flame,
blown into the sky.

Seen from Olympian perspective,
marriage is a slender island, like a wreathe on a
girl's hair:
While the sharp-tailed grouse stomps his dancing
grounds.

A lightness irradiates me like the first taste
of gin.
Dark crystals brightening dancing:
When I fall off the twig it will be without a sound.

The Six-Sided Snowflake

The brown dog trotting out of Painswick
paws sinking into snow pale as water

       & us drifting in our pasts as though we wore our
       parents' clothing, faded now out of fashion.

Elated by cold
I unbolt the door with both hands,
grateful for the freeze and a cinnamon drink inside me.

I move forward with my shadow taupe dog, Depression, in tow.
Six-sided
flakes of the
lace curtains billowing
sugar-dusting streetlamps:
the empty beauty of snow-covered streets reminds me of Tallinn,
    Estonia, St. Petersburg, white nights.
My mood soars. Something will come along to break it.
My girl was calm as I was excited.
A single glass of sake in yet one more empty teahouse.
I pin the organdy curtains where they tore like a bride's tattered gown
    in Mexico or some dusty land where it has miraculously begun
    snowing.

The City Is Wax Combs

Glowing   one lung   two lungs:
with our hiving

taking the imprint of our living.   The North is lonely.
Silk & Bees: buzzing industry.

The greater blue heron, Oriental crumpled feathers, stands on one leg
    smoky gray:
balancing the weight of world & evening.

The beggar rolls on a board with casters: he has no legs. Castration
    caused infection
& his legs had to be amputated.   *See!*

Finally the night will bear the letter with sealing wax which takes the
    missive to you
from me.

All Giving Things

This is the hour
to be glad of all giving things:
Eudora Welty in the world.
Sherry.
Held hands.
This is the hour between dog & wolf
both fanged.
We can bear
having failed in things human
if only we have
the coming home
(ironic, merciful) to these:
mortal,
luminous,
in the night wind.

Seeing Eye

Iris & pupil, dark purple-brown, dilated, the man, the Doukhobor, is
alone as hunger, and goes:
training the winter-thin, water-rippling blond young, golden lab
      the man
      can see into holes of blue ice at
four a.m. that Arctic cold his breath hangs a carved cloud of
      marble before
      him another presence:
he feels both attached to earth & let loose,
more in the mood for Christmas than at Christmas itself.

Now the azure cold bears down, bores in like a drill & settles into
  bone,
      burrowing, an owl:
the cold is bright-blind:

bluer than cobalt,
bluer than indigo.

This Is No Breughel Day

The color is drained from cheeks.
Cows stare from a bleached linen sky:
spiked faces
like saints on the stake
faces whiter than bread
the moon-scarred loaves.
Their faces are a daisy-chain,
raspberry tongues lolling,
running faster than Pieter's pigments,
dumbfounded.
A honed hunter returns from far:
light bag, deep shoulder-scar.

Soon the week will be upon us

like the owl exploding out of the barn
like knight upon peasant

like sack of pippins rolling into cellar
instead of coal   apple-thunder:
bag of white beans split asunder:

one thousand roses massed on the marble
grave
bending the stone.

Soon the sorrow will fly off into the sky like nightjars   into
   snowstorm.

            O

In black boxes, other things will bear down   laces from Flanders
cutting
the bosom   eyelet glass-sharp:
and
like the lighthouse keeper, whose dreams of Icarus
craze & possess him,
his lantern fired in France or Belgium,

       fatally scratched,   fractures
      everywhere the length & breadth of the room   & he
        afire
            where there could be wing behind the scapula
                blazing.

Jeremiah-Weather

Lamentations:
frozen flying wash on the line   pyjamas as flying Dutchmen:
         hours gelled
like panels in a church. We who have been travelling all our lives have
come to pause   like the petrel
   who sleeps on back of the storm:
   like the rose
      opening in intensest heat   in love with her thorn.

Window-washers
(life-risking)   rise in a bright ascension   *Blaze off,*
         washermen!
hooking ladders on sky   white as tether

or buckskin
leather.
They hoick the ladders up, tuck them, like pants into boots, in. *In*
   Memoriam under the World War II Memorial Elms.

○

German units had marched down streets in 1925
during the Great War when the Russians were taken.

Yurts in blizzard
were a stunning
achievement.

Snow for the Slavs & Poles
paralysis for the children who got the virus:
autobiographical.

Jeremiah weather has come & won. Between terribly tall buildings &
   tears
a drift of teal sky appears   rifts the teal, brute & tender, open.

The Hellish Light Or Coppery

The hellish light runs down thru trees
like the charge of bullets thru gunbarrels
strikes bottom
of this once-mining town.
I recall early American windows,
shadows of dollhouse curtains,
Winslow Homers,
neat bookpages turning in the hands.
But there's a breaking of light
from afternoon to evening:
the china blue plate shivering of time
'till we walk about,
living transitions.
We fit tightly in our skin.
Trees unfreeze, the casket's undone.
Chilled but alert as soldiers from the tomb,
one by one the trembling witnesses come.
We're stirring out of the canvas:
colors & varnish cling to our limbs.
We're converting to coal burners.
But these minstrels—
will they ever stop singing?

Civil War Soldier

He raises himself to a razed world: Pre-dawn ash
  sifts.
The Confederate soldier lists . . . the battlefield sways   behind
  his 20-year old bloodshot eyes.

The light exit of the dark   the dark exit of the light
amid the triage workers   he sat up, the wounded man who rose
  & kept rising:
this is the visible insurrection of his invisible death.

Elementary field-surgery
he knows not what lies before him. *Give him two reasons not to die.*

The word rings a bell which tools misery
from the saddest part of his childhood:
he looked down the ward like looking down a gunbarrel to Hell.

All those carts unfolded like extinct cranes dusted off
brought from some dark museum vault: sprung open for children.

The children lay in cots
as men did now: some being carried out on gurneys with wood
  handles:
a nest of others suffering: like eggs, like Russian dolls.

The week in Purgatory.
Medieval weights & pulleys.

His own mother would prefer him to die:
The fine planed wood doors of heaven sliding, waxed & oiled,
  opening.

Now's hallucination:
the naily river of rehabilitation   on its banks the wounded &
  dying: bandages no longer white but blood-stained & gray:

when body habits another house, in the body & sharp, but a great
   change comes.

   Pain. Amputation.
         The cracking of bone
          brings the entire light down like a revolving wheel, ceiling
to crack & shatter his remaining bones:
   not Michelangelo's Sistine
   despite the scaffold he's swaying on   like he's drunk a fifth
   of Jim Beam:
   no Southern Comfort in the bled light leans
   like a dying soldier upon his stick:
   a bladed tool he turns, helplessly, dazzled, shocked in his hands.

Firstborn / Lastborn

Soon the apple festival will come
and the world will be
normal as boys.

I was the child who took our mother's heart
out of her
chest.

A blonde gypsy rail-thin boylong girl.
The second down had olive skin.
Only father's last born

bore the same Latvian
look
& coloring

and she became
the physician
his woman in white. Spare table. Second wife. Dark light. Bright salt.

Zap Mama acapella.
Your life runs on & on like a stream on a silver pitcher, dented,
dimpled with the years.

Who rode the rail of our hope
boxcar full of flowers & songs?
Who didn't stand near the third rail most of the time?

There was never a time
when Yom Kippur
fasting & grieving didn't seem redundant.

What a Waste Of World

> *Yesterday Mother still drew*
> *Sleep toward them like a white moon,*
> *There was the doll with cheeks de-rouged*
> > *by kisses*
>
> Nelly Sachs, "O the Night Of the Weeping
> Children!" from O the Chimneys,
> translated by Michael Hamburger

i.
Bleeding Thru the Roses On Your Quilted Vest

O Lord of burning, how permit *this* conflagration?

At intervals through day, glancing at sun through barbed wire birds,
Bergie, you brusht the hair from your eyes, thin as smoke or nerves.

Fifty springs ago, you were a girl opening a new cake of lustrous rosin.
At *Yom Kippur* air was flammable kerosene.
Then you were taken
rounded up.

O

This, walking from the beginning,
your shoes ripped off your feet:
the outer world harsh, the inner not forgiving.

White out love's name;   snow had fallen during night.
It was in brick crevices
of this star-shaped fortress
which was your hell:
a trio was rehearsing chamber music.
Despite the music, despite the theatre, despite the dancing
it was all a macabre theatre, aglitter
like that snow world at the Town Gate of Nuremburg

into which Casper Hauser came.
You too had been stabbed to the heart
bleeding
through the roses on your quilted vest.

ii.
Closing Both Eyes You Imagined

Bleeding thru the roses on your quilted vest,
closing both eyes you imagined   first snow back home
mirror-like
flake after flake
six-sided
spinning
dizzily
melting:
language, speech forming, before you lost them
&
the triage workers came.

Old Father, his pipes & leathers, old Mother, her yarns of colors,
their names will be written in the Book of Life.
You had no sweethearts, only Lisi, little sister: you were too young
to have lain with a boy.

Theresienstadt

> *There are stones like souls*
> Rabbi Nachman

Were *those* stones once souls   of the small fortress?
Star-shaped   thick-walled
with the cypress like rows of black torches:
"the paradise of the camps."

Even the Red Cross was duped   into thinking this was a spa.
This once military prison sucking souls from the shtetls.

The winds form a gallows:
gray, vaulted, cloisters.   daring to mimic a church
from which to watch the humans
melt away.

             O

Parting hours like grasses   or the part in a child's hair.
People like Bergie know shops are back there in the village: cereal &
    tea.
Here the air is granular   grains of ice, which rub flesh till it
    bleeds.
These dough-pale hours.

There was Martha   there Sabine, Marie:
They walk   exhaling fragile breath, which leaves a small cloud
upon the air
soon sharpening whiter & whiter
      as though their *Bas Mitzvah* dresses
         have been exchanged for burial robes.

Look once
down the gray stone well & you will never look again:

but look away from the reflections
which ice will seal over
>	like the happiness of our people
>	driven into permanent exile
>	to reflect like copper branches
>	in iridescent ice, hallucinatory, frozen.

Help My Unbelief

Help my unbelief,   guide me along on the medieval wooden crutch
     of faith, a stilt
moving on rooflines: hand on the banister of memory
which has constructed a small spiral staircase outside the main house.

It is like war
sky an endless lemon-gray
on the brink of rain which never comes.

As long as we deny our past
we are mutilated:
we suffer a missing part, an amputation

or become two personalities in one.
I recall a cradle & in another life entering a bombed church with
frieze of stars and angels pelted by rain.

A forced vagabondage.
Loess soil.
The darker aspects of military life flashed upon my girlhood

ending up in a destroyed pharmacy
small glass cabinets
broken glass-paned cabinets, bottles dust-covered.

Somber clarity,
thick layers of ice in the wash-basin when I wake.
Ice on the stoop: a commotion of frost-flowers in the milkbottles
     luminous cobalt like steel.

Houses with missing panes so snow will blow in.
Sappers gut homes
taking planks & beams to reinforce their bunkers.

And always endless rows of convoys coming.
Carrying oxygen.

brassy yellow sun on the dawn horizon. Despair.

Many makeshift lights in darkness
long shadows
a Rembrandt look.

One foot planted in life
one in death.
How to proceed?

And always the exhaustion of war
the convoys
yellow lamps blotter-smudged with dirty fog.

Peasoup-green.
A commutation of a death sentence.
Cannabis flames. Cerulean sky.

Amen.
Nocturnal gossip among nurses
changing shifts. Elation for them, sinking gut-level depression for the
    children whose hurly burly is done.

I see the fabled Russian winters
in these cots I swear
kids' blue lips moving with a message, a sigh

women carrying birdcages
out of ruined homes.
Roads and snow.

Shades of Turgenev
Farewell. Farewell.
It adds up. One knows nothing.

The hood on a raven
the caw of a rook black bleak clothespin:
star-gazing, numbed out, I call you Nurse Littlejohn:

I slept on what used to be a cabinet.
An angel in the snow
fallen from a cornice, her eye scarred with char.

Being bathed under tall tall ceilings which are not religious
and skylights
is humiliating.

In North Ossetia two years later
the crisis center, it is discovered,
remained directionless for twenty-four hours when the school was
    sabotaged by Chechens.

Search forces used
flame-throwers
which caused the school gym roof to collapse.

Superimposed upon hurricane victims
scant relief in the South,
I see a jambalaya indeed of the deeply live, the deeply dead.

(Help thou my unbelief
for I am
stumbling.)

Meanwhile the carrying goes on & on:
stirrings
hard-won,

so much shadow plunging the ward into gray
one hardly notices the dead child small as a doll borne out
parallel with the horizon.

Short Visiting Hours For Children

Short Visiting Hours For Children

These Noddies have nothing else to wait for
but God will make no intercession;
so why are visiting hours so short cut by razors
when pain is a dominant extension:
stretched out white winter snake
or the braids Mother used to loop around her finger
our shining copper,
chestnut,
lustre like new butter?

Children lined on stretchers in halls
reminiscent of the Civil War drummers &
soldier boys with guns, aged 14:
girls ephemeral in white down aisles like a nunnery, 9, 10, 11.
O Convent:
Covenant:
white bedsteads with the whirlpool of vacant white air
spinning beside them a top in
an abyss.
Vortex open & up
over a metal cup.
The void wheels in small circles of steamed milk.
There was a childhood left behind:
flower coming out of cracks in the sidewalk.
Now the red & the white corporals are drawn from the vial
gunning, warring.

The flocked lamb simply fell out of my arms.
Loss struck like a fist
like the Wonderful Wallendas on their final demonstration;
the hours of the Mothers & Fathers came & went down stairs like
    choirboys carrying candles:
the mirrors reflected them

the poor hours
when a whirlpool suctioned
autumn rain
& teal ice,
glazier of Chylde Winter's tomb, came.
Why, when all was so brief, shorn, puny & the will of the matron iron-
    strong,
why were visiting hours not more long?

Multiplication

   How can I be wheeled down these white corridors
23 years after, without touching your hand, brightening, diminishing:
   tawny-girl in lace cap of sunlight:
movement without memory is insanity: you are planted in tapestry:
   a cobalt flower?

   Your 12-year-old hands held the reins
of death surely, your eye aflame:
   while cancer went about its multiplication
exact as lace, or honeycomb.

   They cut off one leg
but it reached the hip:
   indigo wore you down.
(We'd close our eyes to picture cobalt-gardens.)

   Your cheeks some days were bone-white
like the girl of Dresden holding our silk lampshade
   back home:
other days, they were pink like those planted in quilts:

   Rose, a North Renaissance girl,
near the close of your life
   your face was pearl: Milky-gray,
it glowed in all that brightness by the window:

   a nun of 12, determined, not angry,
whose sole task was to meet your king.
   Cobalt-gardens multiplied, then. A sole visitor,
an aunt brought you a fur-trimmed jacket for your diminished frame.

   You grew up three years overnight, & were a Vermeer
young woman: (the Dutch wear such jackets in wintertime
   to keep out the damp cold of Delft Holland)
the windowpane threw lemon light on your jacketed frame.

   Hoarfrost formed in the glass —
multiplying, multiplying, until by ice-tables, they covered
   you & me both with lace of a cream-white curtain
celled by snowflake bright incarceration.

Opaque disease

        or transparent?
The bullet bee thrums above the rose.

The drone hovers.
     But the bone alone knows
whether it multiplies or diminishes.

Darkly-wise
       like church pews after nightfall
the cell doors close.

Cubicle-mate:
       your furious gentleness is gone
who nourished yourself upon wafers of flesh, iron, bone.

But the life-force
       is will: still glowing, steel
drawn forth by dark tongs.

Sister—twin—
       we were separated by a parchment partition
till sun poured thru that charred honeycomb:

     Fire & air were one at the end.

Time taken at the flood

New York City, Winter, 1951

   doesn't   lead to fortune:
      blackflies stick to yellow paper
            curling from the ceiling.   In jam for our
tea.

Terraces of Bellevue   (like water-terraces in Nepal)
        overflowed: whole families carried in.
          Lawns were set up with crude cots—with
              whatever mystic comfort the sick take from
the presence of doctors & nurses.

Apothecary & a prayer.
Fireworks in wool.
The medallion sweater   for that first weekend
trees of Manhattan just dipped in frost's flame.
Sun, a fiery winter ball dropped by wrecker into the Hudson.

Heart casing breaking up   like ice floes on the river   a shattered
   crystal
                                          boat:
      when we took up life again,   it was by the throat.

Buckled

The spoon buckled & blistered.
The glue stuck to the wrong side.
The map was bent beyond boundaries.
It woke you from a dream, plunged your hand in blue:
life
about-faced when your child rose
with leukemia
and gazed out the window.
The backyard:
Its agate shone like a battleship.
It was up to you now to scale the snow
in buckets of shadows
the tin roof beating
in the Arctic.
The Tundra Bakery lit up,
teens ganging there Saturday night.
As if she had outgrown life, the garment grew too thin.
Your ears were ripped off like jackals' in the wind:
mica. The sinew & shrapnel of bringing a child into the world.
Quick sparks flew from the spur of the moon.
A daughter taken into time:
face fixed to the wind as to the mirror,
stars for hair. Or the bird plunging in.

Unroped

Sickness in those days was a special place, a place apart, where no one else could enter, not the doctor with his shiver-inducting stethoscope or even . . . mother
       John Banville, The Sea

Let go your Lenten life. Grey ice like a moss
the old green velvet wedding dress
for a ceremony conducted at the Justice of the Peace.
What Peace?

A *louche* world? You were both fond & rueful.

A lawful bride,
but in an heirloom light saved, spun long ago:

now
let the calm in
at the end the camera very close, almost forgiving.

What was
sad, small, why fight so for it? First the hip broke like a fragile cup
then your iron will mellowed
now pneumonia
in that lung scarred by cancer long ago. You were younger than I
am now.

The die cast, the dice thrown, the snow monkey
lemon-white as meringue
with the bravado of a toreador's cape
open the shutters pushed out from that darkest of all hospital
wings,
the mental wing where little ever changes

            let sun
spill upon ivory bone: cross the Mercy, no longer fearful but
                daringly
      open your heirloom courage
          spun by generations
    cover your shoulders with its shawl

         your thin backbone
              easing,
       muscles coming unroped:
    feel the wreathe of stars blazing on.

I Wish To God Your Depression Were a Lake

Frozen teal   iced reflecting Netherlandish sky
clouds the hue of the sugar a mule carries
the snow the monkey is named after.
I would skate, circling it to rim like seventeenth century canals in
   Holland lined with brick houses
bell rooves
step rooves.
I'd climb and ring a bell
in the highest one.
I'd have it in the palm of my mind.

I cannot get my brain around it:
I picture sunrise rimming a frozen pond,
or an axe which can chop
into iridescent square school-houses & choir-churches of ice.

The harrowing of hope has paid its tuition.
Your depression is a closed wooden box with smallest breathing-hole.

Hawsers & hooks:
Anglo-Saxon words I'd make workhorses to drag offal to another city
at distant perimeter to us:
that the dark refuse be given bright burning.

Pneumonia

Pneumonia　　　　　　tangles in the blue branches, lung tissue
　　inflamed:
an old person's friend.

Maybe one gets a virus in one lung & like George Straight when he
　　puts on his hat it's all over.

What would be nice to be carried out in?
The Silver Stream parked under an elm like an inflated oval balloon,
scents of old hays mingling with leathers?

Or the box of ice crushed silver-blue?

A scattering of salts?
She always took to the ink-black moon.

All I could think of if I were her was going out for a walk in the stir:
　　　stirrups, ice, gray & metal wind.

Down the street is a Chinese place which serves won ton floating like
　　lilies in a pond.

Tobacco was the fix till cancer scraped & scarred one lung.
Vodka?
Lit matches with woman friends.
The seductive book.

Conversation burns low with hardly a visible flame.

She's always been on both side of the Berlin wall.

Eleven P.M. She dreads that hour
when self-destruction beckons,
the moon white as a wedding cake,
a loaf of soap,
heartless, ancient as the Great Wall of China
visible from its craters.

Second Notification

You could be in the ward: you could be in the morgue:
you could be on the same   page with death.   Sounds &
    furious stars rolling overhead   spilling with apple-thunder.
We haven't heard.
But we're second notification.

    If the broken man caught you,
    you forgot your promise
    to cling to the brass bedpost in extremity.

First will be brother, beloved, doctors
friends:
last, frost telling loss to the garden in syllables lost in translation.

100%

Field-mice, like stones, dormant:
it was war. No butter. Rations bitter.
And always & forever winter.

Now, steep earth, love ceiling:
rowing with Anne, cabin-fever, ribcage aching after radiation
oars over torn water, slipped into oar-locks, put paid to healing.

They are trying a new chemical

in her cocktail
red as cockscomb:
fiery as barn
burning,
a hexagonal one.
The air's the color of old tea stains,
ironing-board triangles:
"Lesbia" (she thinks) "*Sappho & Sandalwood, where are you
    gone?*"

You have started up this foxy engine

linking me with you again:
my carbine: blue, boxed breathing machine,
now going on oxygen, a glower in a jar
violet:
dragging about the pad.
I care not that the violas wear hoods, nor that the frost hangs
between branches of trees
white fog
sculptural
surreal:
like coal in boxcars:
O
sitting under a New Orleans bridge one night
crying about being stabbed.
Like the magical boy, perpetual child, you cast no shadow:
your bones define thinness
as your lavish spirit spills images, copious: cornucopia, horn of
    plenty:
defines expense: the spent fuel of a mile and a half long coal train
thru the mountains
and over the plain:
coming into this apple-green American vigil of a dawn.

Make hay while the sun shines

hue & tint of Vermeer's yellow flowers   old leather gloves
    butter.
Let us leave the issue of dying: one can find oneself by the
    moon:
besides, you are a bit curious about the other side
after all these years of passion for the green planet we're on
with the golden ricks on old, wintering air.

You might have hidden under the crawl-space of mother's house.
Gray clock-mouse. Gash on the cheek.   But you fell in love with
    a linguist
whose death tore the tongue out of grieving.
You might have sat under a Mississippi bridge & cried all night
years after your husband
died of tainted cow brains
with a man who cried too. He overcame his wound; you never did.
While your husband was out often when young,
you went watering the glass
till you could see thru it   purity & surprise, putting
    Nantucket in your raincoat
pocket.

Your world is
re-visioned   *inwarding*:
rain will soon dot the dark pool. You arch like a cat your spine:

waters flow under the bridge of your body
gymnast:
you cull longing, spool it. Lick the cream of dream-
relations.

Night is the color slate-roof with soapstone sheen.
The truck rolls thru town:
"Who's keeping you warm?" Columbia Fuels.

This recurrence
is a result of your being in poverty:
the truck blew up, you could not go for monthly checkups.

That check bounced.
It's been canceled.
But you've kept your rendezvous with the gods, the ones who haven't
    been betrayed
by time.

If I could implant *this* village with *these* clouds curved like swan's
neck behind your eye the way ocular implants come
from Clearwater, Florida . . .

No way.
Inverno:
winter: Let us cut our losses at this.

Ice-sculpture: I watch circling Pacific Mobile Veterinary Station.
One goes alone toward the alone.
The dark air goes down & a cry goes up, out of sight like a parachute:
reverse-motion.

Shaker Box, Broom, Clock

> *How did a sect so small make objects so sublime?*
> Adam Gopnik, "The Shining Tree Of Life," *New Yorker*, February 2006

nob on clock   faces,
the cult of box & broom,
Docent

trifles make perfections but perfection is no small thing.

Capsized with that step-daughter of cancers, the lung
which the doctors shrug
"I told you so."
You flee Hurricane Rita to arrive at a sister's in Austin
one lung left
one child grown
one canister of portable oxygen.

The drumbeat repetition of the heart,
objects that look like objects roll call of ordinary mornings,
the knock of eggs boiling in a pot,

a last long echo of the childhood
makes you shudder:
abused, outcast, girl-child by the barn:
echoes
sketched by a Seer
whom you studied: Blake's drawing:

the practicality of it all:
the improbability of your cruel
spill

you could share with no one:

an underlying hysteria
preventing your taking your life
but taking poetry by the throat rather
and stroking those mystical gorge-feathers into song.

Living On One Lung

i.

Braving it out in Austin with kin also ill, suffering: brother-in-law
    paraplegic, with seizures & brain damage
your own
ravaged chest takes Blues air in.

Think of a meteorologist
working alone in a small weather office:
you in your improvised bedroom in a sister's living room turned
    office, computer-room, sickroom

carrying oxygen from room to room
the one lung delicate as a violet.

ii.

The ward sharpened my eyes
gave me my focus: became my telescope   at twelve
to render tears and the sorrow.

iii.

If I could turn myself inside-out
you would see an abandoned theme park   rollercoasters,
    loup-de-loup & tunnel of horrors
in heavy snow, with icicles, where childhood stood.

Winters homebound
windows warmed with old blankets, wind whistling round West End
    Ave. and Broadway:
copper geraniums, tatty orange velvet like tatty music scores, moth-
eaten bindings.

Eblouissant.
Stunning.

iv.

The beloved phones her computer text consultant
I phone the hospital
where Mother is

living the past quarter year.   I read Lowell to re-enter New England
sparkling darkly like rock-candy:
helping her go out not in defeat but in style.

You with one lung remaining, are learned   always did everything in
 style:
smoked
read, learned Russian, wore hats.

 They were playing the wrong opera when I walked into the room.
 Homer was blind paraphrasing Latin. But work won.

  Cold foxes bark at edge of day.
  What are we together? What in separation?

 Eyelids lift, let in a draft of heaven.

Hollyhock

It takes you ten minutes these days to remember the word
    "Hollyhock."

After being sick 6 ways to Sunday,
you have clear eyes.
I see the bruised blue vein where the IV was
infusing scarlet chemicals
for hours
against lungs filled with tumors which took me back to the
    planetarium.

Kate, all you wanted to return to, like Dickinson, was your carved
    paper box
for poems.
A hinge of paper
a shelf of sand.

You spoke the purest tongue: Almost Elizabethan.
Lost horses dotting your horizon
like stray figures   wandered out of the Globe figure
from Shakespeare's time:
"Holly," "Hock," hock a holly, trade in a blue flame
while shepherds guard above their question marks of canes
into the present age
taking by the throat
the grain
that carved the note
dissonant,
dissident.
If it takes you ten hours to remember the word for the flower
    "Hollyhock"
I'll cock my ear
I'll be listening,
listening.

Rembrandt's Smock

When Winter Comes

(for Jackson Wheeler)

Each April evening is the color of some flower:
lilac, bluebell, hawthorn.
Autumn?
Nightfalls become mahogany:
maple, cedar.

But when Winter comes,
it's impossible to pinpoint colors:
nightfalls are
colors of slowly-healing scars.

Try
"file-dark"
hues that tip a brush, painting Byzantine Icons:
more violent, flaming tints than one would use to paint St. Francis.

When ice comes, hues challenge a Brueghel:
Medieval
copper, bronze, silver, golds beaten:
each blue determined by
shape & hue
of Setting Sun.

O

When Winter comes, it's
isolation of survivors. So take the hand
to fuse the bond
throwing sparks, welding, then moving on.

Lithograph Of Amherst

> *Agony enacted there*
> *motionless as peace*
> Emily Dickinson

This calm ribbon of air
    is
a lost language lesson.

Towns
    like etchings under glass
resemble this one.

Day's profile
    is arrested
arrogant, precise.

Footprints
    are covered
by leaves & ice.

Time irons
    pressmarks
& bubbles in.

Color is borne home
    the hue of birds' wings
the hue of old bone.

        O

Fate stopped
    at this desk, this town:
the shining black inkwell. Then moved on.

A Few Canvases

I prop
on the easel
skeletal north light pouring in

two seascapes:
one cream-white cluster
of mums

a single lithograph of town. What town?
How long? Dressed in black, I'm safe, chaste,
nite-lite on at noon, sparrow in her nest.

Perfectly balanced, forever strange.
North sea light gives best reading, for all it wanes.
Finally,

a room like Dickinson's.
If severe, it is because

the moon can be a candle at noon:
sun at midnight.
War raging—that candle

flames brightest which illumines
not *thee* or *me*—but a few bright lines:
these leap like tallow

dangerously
white
to burn.

Burning with a mineral-brightness
all night   in the mind.

This Wired World

This wired world
is where we love.   Outside the box
poems   droves   of them come like covered wagons from
     dark canvas   skies   where in spades   it rains.

I'd want my last morning to be precisely like this one:
an October sky   gleaming:
Death an empty mirror   where no cart is.

*Cocksure,
swaggart braggadocio   big brain*
the world cracks down.   This bleak richness is pauper
    haven.

The geometers
have finally met
Vermeer.

               Gone are
               John Constable's knotty landscapes
               fog used like chamois   to wipe with alcohol the
               silver, pearled globe whistle-clean.

Photographs Of Albatrosses

Reading an article
this phrase stops me short, "photographs of albatrosses."
Is it plural?
I rarely see us as one, but more rarely as two:
stronger than coupled,
richer than individuals.
I see the amethyst geode struck open
& at the same time, I envision the yield
of albatrosses spilled
into the sky with pearl light all around them:
mystical
blessed-omen bird.

O

You think you are unheard
but you are heard.
I think I fall behind
but am ahead
who soon may see geraniums
as rich explosions of red-orange
who may shoot beyond this range.
What then?
It was a long time coming on
& may never be gone:
it is part & parcel
of my earthly living: tissue, blood & lens:
the endangered species
fly over
as the loss of them threatens,
& autumn deposits a bloom
on flowers, barns, all things:
& each of us is delivered that vehicle of vision & wisdom:
Film.

Brightwork / Ave

I give you this: Brightwork:
the birds' breasts embroidered with
dew like dye.

The tapestry finch & the real, teal one
too—singing
during the gravedigger's shift.

Pearled rain
on the rim of the night watchman's
hat.

Give you fields
frosted
like drawings for an illustrated botany from the last century: tracing
     paper windows protecting them.

I give the war plants   where guns were manufactured, & ammunition.
Give frozen
these plants from the air, like dead flowers on the ground.

Ave
Maria Purissima.
I sang all the way to Flatbush—& back into Manhattan.

Wheeling in circles
out front
frosted breath, breaking an orange open with bare hands.

Yule was round the bend:
phantom-jets thundered above cloudline.

I have proffered you this: words.
Travel. Unravel. Ave.

Though I chain you to this earth each day:
I tender you this white-knuckled labor, brightwork to do. . . Ave.

Danish geese,

              behind glass in a Dutch museum, the tour-guide,
young,
unfolds notes in his hand;

streets of Delft unpleat.
Silence, like calyx enfolds flower, enfolds him:
Rue Marchand becomes parchment crackling under the tour guide's voice
with a few scar-burns:
fire thru an instrument.   Astonishment.

Pausing at each sentence close   just long enough to let sun thru
Dutch door   upper half holds cobalt evening
canals at street-tips throbbing like temple-veins.

Bringing the tower-ravens in

in crystalline February in London   could bode
bad fortune   shining over us,   around to all sides like shaken
         black silk:
over our poet's imagination   in the ozone & oxygen:
it shimmers in   cold clear Lenten light.
The raven master has had to bring
the ravens in
in mirror-like freeze.

Tragedy may come overnight upsetting the whole apple cart;
red pippins spilled like coal down the cellar-chute.

What is raven, what his cold clock?

A birth
peeling off when memories of the half-known
         surface chill and
         the eye, the mind scrapes like visors   ice from Breughel's teal.

Lady Luck is down on us. Ill fortune is shining over us
cold clear.

The ravenmaster has had to bring
the two, the pair of rosin-glossy, pitch pine
ravens, a tradition for centuries, in
like copper nails rusting
from the roof of the tower of London
and cage them.

Horsefall Backward Slow Motion

It is not apocalypse.
Stroke by stroke
it is you
like a great sculpture of twelve years in mottled stone
rising
becoming airblown
all the particles
like a Seurat painting
—ankle to knee
mending,
knee to elbow
clots healing
or undone
the bright knots of ruby in the sun.

A week before, the horses had been sunbathing.
You moving upward from green
earth
in astonishing

slowness;
each tone & timbre
of earth brushed into skinned hand, arm

immensely light & heavy at one time
as if mounting
air

your chestnut hair
streaming before you
like reddish water

making you temporarily blind
till hands find
touch of warm hide, & leather again:
putting the world back in balance

which was curved
in a fastball

coming down
on you
despite helmet.

It's left you with thirsting touch
searching gaze
for an earth to graze easily again.

It was everything over:
in a waterfall, a rush—
or else regain the reins, the wind.

Boy With Ball

Autumn brings a buzz of children's voices;
a toss of color
darkens ground
a moving shadow
burned by a red fire pump
like the bouquet the bride throws over her shoulder
and who catches it?
Or bird seed
or wild rice confetti.
Like *Boy with Ball*
India-ink on oat-yellow
life's spectral.

Here above the 49th parallel
it's gritty, gusty.
Old nicotine light proliferates:
that particular sepia sun distilled in photography studios at turn-of-
 century
or brown, doctors' waiting rooms: Light italicizes autumn.

Boy with Ball:
Black & yellow sign
the exact colors of a bee
and he has his sting. See
he's drawn the moment before hand paddles ball:
you think he has it all

but his legs end without feet
only
yellow ground on which he seemingly runs   miraculous
 like Jesus or the boy in the orthoptics stick glass when I was
 young & cross-eyed.

No stumps even.
No war amp: but a child: and he has this wild deforming: most times you don't notice. That is because what sign deleted
           the mind paints in.

Frost Flowers

        i.

A scrim covers the brown parlor.
when the earth moves, *"Run to the hills,"* cry earthquake children.

I wake, scrape a layer of ice:
frost flowers emerge, eerie, geometric as Euclid's surface:
Gesualdo fills the canvas of our home from top to bottom
family music echoing
taking refuge in rafters: white echoes mingle with sombre ones.

        ii.

When the entire hockey rink is an ice shield under northern night,
rink-workers bring a zamboni in.

I sigh over the blind kid closing a sleepy eye;
over the chill
layering glass cables carrying messages from Palestrina Street
glowing like the Aurora Borealis.
There, like the Talmud stands the black glossy Steinway:

I will play pity on it & old hymns.

Blood was red Mississippi daybreak

noon butter-yellow as Iowa
all the wheat waving, by night inked over.

Chalk storms
blew
obliterating Kansas farms.

Strife
struck the family
misfortune like July lightning after a day made in heaven, blue ingot
pouring voltage of cobalt:

        forked, it struck: astounding us lulled into illusive
           calm:
        angling over Quaker wheat, Shaker barn
        burning the whole design in the brain
                before bringing the loft & news,
                  the mews of wrought iron
                    all the way down
                      to Cinder Town.

When you consider that freedom is an illusion

dwelling even in the New South, & how —
at our separate screens in twilight as in the highest boughs of an
    appletree
                                      in spring when we were
                                              children—
we are happy. I ask—

did one ever really walk across
a courtyard in Berlin?
Holding consciousness, a red precarious lantern?

On a winter's night
we go to that
blue glow: An igloo, as though that will fulfill us now.

When you consider the gladiators of love,
my sister,
it seems like a dream, your back pain:

you can't push the river & I can't pull
you here:
you never chose to come back:

Still, flickering behind my screen I can see the fierce adoration
of the ethereal
androgynous child.

When I consider
that it all may be an illusion
why do I tremble & lift it so gingerly as if my hands had found
                                                  the crack in the
                                                         world

& the whole evening might shatter
like fractured paperweight snowball bleeding white into my hands.

Rembrandt's Smock

Cobalt   bending glass   ominous translucent light of Rotterdam
small deaths of his
children   long visiting hours at the grave:

the crack in the globe
thru which
the dark shone.

A thin window stands before him
giving onto brick
a concave mirror in his background:

one thin red foxes traveled earth
thru flame:
one silver spilled from glass & in canals ran.

Once it was a bolt
of measured   blue-
black cloth   the smock. Now that

rooks took
Northern Europe,
blond wheat stacks   stooks   surge & sear whitegold flame.

None of it
contained the cobalt the indigo ocean
washing within him

billowing
swirling   but
his smock caught reflections

which gathered clouds before snow
storm   which broke:
enfolding him   black tulip.

Some nights   he hangs it on no nail but it wraps him   he goes to
    sleep in
exhausted
by his easel   (his apprentice Tulp, a lost dream). The painter

wakes
eyes burning
poor sleep   nightmares   broken bleak black steeds
    stale day-old bread

to paint again & again
the Jew
of Rotterdam.

○

Rembrandt's smock
a snow bank
black in night   caved in   hanging him in effigy:

a shock of wildwheats
blended
in pockets from summer.

The crack in the world thru which the light shone: buried
    his barely born kinder.
Turpentine. Linseed in nostrils, lungs,
In old age   there are the huge canvases cut up. Kneeling on the
icy stone floor to sell small ones, he works

for folk
to patch
holes in their draughty Holland kitchens.

He paints a smock
puff sleeves   round collar   older Titus, still a boy, a virgin:
his one son   who lived.

Rembrandt
sleeps, the painter   in his paint: tints, hues, dyes, pigments:
Oils, umbers, argents pressed into his bones.

He will rise in blackness   before dawn
to offer cursory prayer
drink bitter coffee grinds.

Death
penury
debt climb heaven before him, a cloud.   The Plagues, quarantines
    bypassed him, the Black Death which followed one from home
    to home   canal to canal.

Behind   him surges
a pack
of hounds.

A chorus of charcoal voices
a
chorale rises

the sketch,
carbon   under his fingernails darkness of altos in choirs
in his ribs,   takes shape:

pastels
soft as Sunday morning's egg
sky hard as thorns.

        O

Hollow the box of collection coin   Hellish
on Sundays passed round
like a bird with broken wings.   Congregants cast eyes down.

A wood box
panel
slid open.   Abacus beads of his spine creak, a February morning.
    Sky the color of burnished leather.

○

His eyes glass over. One could take
worn chamois
to fashion a horse, doll for the boy or girl.

The color
of the eyes of the Jews
what to make of them?

A
galaxy
of stars.

Saskia is rising, plump breasts spilling out of green satin bodice:
Titus in his beret, crush hat, impress of the father's copper eyes, is
    stirring. Sky like porridge.
North light like great boats frozen in harbor ice cracking like thunder
    of guns.

Black
beret velour
contours belong to boyhood still beautiful as a girl

but it's his sun
radiating
like thorns in the crown of Christ   throwing spike light into
    corners, caressing all things.

Antwerp
Amsterdam

Utrecht

medieval towns
changed with the changing northern light,
blush

of color in cheeks left for the girl.
But the smock
he slipped on each morning   once a bolt of coarse cloth   now is
    silk with colors:

its countries
swirls of oil
linseed turp

pressed
some nights
pitch him into dreams   like a pitchfork thrusting hay into a fire.

Foghorns
pierce
a Dutch winter: a shaft of old gold sun pierces his heart like the
    pearl the girl's ear. His smock

it enfolded
refolded
him each

Dutch morning
despite   Death   Debt   Penury   the cold
the only enfold —
ment   (Tulp, his apprentice, a frozen dream   under ice
his blueish-lips)
the crack in the globe that let   *shine sin & sun*
sombre

    the deepest call   culling,   coloring   lung breath drawn deep
    to sign the linen.

About the Author

Lynn Strongin was born in New York City in 1939. Her childhood, with its rich Russian-Jewish cultural background, was filled with music, painting, and theatre. Lynn's early studies in piano led her to the Manhattan School of Music's musical composition program, while her younger sister Martha became a concert violist and founding member of the Cleveland Quartet. Strongin transferred to Hunter College when she realized that music alone could not convey what she wanted to say, and began her studies in literature and poetry. She has won a National Endowment for the Arts Creative Writing Grant, two PEN grants, and received four Pushcart Prize nominations.

Strongin has published eleven books of poetry, and has had work in over twenty anthologies; her work appears in numerous North American and European print and online journals and has been translated into Italian, French, and German. Her anthology, The *Sorrow Psalms: A Book of Twentieth Century Elegy* was published by the University of Iowa Press in 2006. Her most recent poetry books include *Dovey & Me* (Solo Press: 2006), *The Birds of the Past Are Singing* (Cross-Cultural Communications: 2006) and *The Girl with Copper-Colored Hair* (Conflux Press, forthcoming).

www.ingramcontent.com/pod-product-compliance
Lightning Source LLC
Chambersburg PA
CBHW071024080526
44587CB00015B/2492